MANIFEST YOUR DREAMS

*Learn to Manifest Your Every Desire
With The Law of Attraction*

Lisa Julie

Disclaimer

The entire rights of the content found in this e-Book are reserved with the publisher. The replication or republication of any part of this content in any possible form is strictly prohibited without getting the consent from the author of the book. Any such action that comes to the notice of publisher is punishable by law.

This e-book is solely for educational purposes and should be taken as such. The author takes no responsibility for any misappropriation of the contents stated in this e-book and thus cannot and will not be held liable for any damages incurred because of it.

TABLE OF CONTENTS

Introduction 5
Chapter 1: What is the Law of Attraction 7
Chapter 2: The Law of Attraction and Religion 11
Chapter 3: How the Law of Attraction Works..........15
Recap Chapters 1, 2, 3..27
Chapter 4: Resistance 29
Chapter 5: Training Your Vibration and Attraction....49
Conclusion 55
Recap of Chapters 1-5..57

Workbook..59
Exercise One: Living In The Now 61
Exercise 2: Staying in A Neutral State 63
Exercise 3: Staying in your Vibration 65
Exercise 4: Effortless Manifestation 67
Exercise 6: Timing..69
Conclusion 71
FAQs page...73
Final Words...79

INTRODUCTION

*"What you are is what you have been.
Who you will be is what you do now."*
- **Buddha**

*C***ongratulations**! You have actively shown the Universe that you are ready to learn. This is not a gift or a coincidence or even a reward. Yes, those words echo all that you have been told about how the Universe or God works and that if you are good you receive a reward or maybe the Universe is "teaching us a lesson" and last but not least that it is all "meant to be".

Be prepared, that in the next chapters you will begin to let go of those notions and beliefs but not have to let go of your personal religious and philosophical beliefs. You are learning Quantum Physics here. You are learning how the mechanics of matter and the Universe—your personal Universe works.

So, what will you learn by reading this book that you've attracted at just the right time?

- **Getting everything you want effortlessly**

- **Learning the secret that has been kept from us by the ruling 1% of the world**

- **Become a powerful influencer and influence the people around you by example**

- **Never EFFORT for anything again**

- **Never doubt yourself and never beat the drum of negative thoughts again**

This is just the beginning and only a fraction of what you will come away with. This will no doubt be the most valuable—life-changing book you'll ever read.

It's not just a book—it's an experience.

CHAPTER 1

What is the Law of Attraction

"The Law of Attraction states that whatever you focus on, think about, read about, and talk about intensely, you're going to attract more of into your life."
- Jack Canfield

This seems the only logical place to start in telling you what the Law of Attraction really is and why on earth it is called a "Law". Let's begin by using a simple example, for instance, the Law of Gravity. It is called a "Law" because it is something constant and unwavering. It cannot be changed. If I am carrying an apple in my hand and I drop it, it must hit the ground. This, in the history of man on this planet has not changed.

The same goes for the "Law of Attraction". This is just as real a Law as is gravity but—it is not readily accepted by mainstream science as gravity because face it—there is less hard proof in our daily lives for the "Law of Attraction" than the "Law of Gravity".

That is unless you are "awake" and "aware" of the Law. People see it in their lives daily and still call them coincidences or even blessings. And while there is nothing wrong with this—they will benefit so much more to have really know what it is and how to "work it" in their lives.

Explaining the Law of Attraction:

The "Law of Attraction" is best explained in lay terms as examples. You may first recognize it as being "coincidence" or even "synchronicity" and while you would be correct to an extent—when the Law is truly understood—*it is so much more.*

Examples:

So many people have learned the art of "visualization". It helps to an extent at least to put you in the mindset of what you need to do. However, if you notice not much other than that happens. Then you have those people walking around that have everything go right and everything just fall into place. Most of the time those people know what is popularly called "The Secret" without having seen the actual movie "The Secret". You may want to look it up after you finish this book, by the way.

We digress—back to the example. The difference between the people that have these situations fall into place the way they visualized it is they will place the most important ingredient into the mix which is "Emotion". Now, it sounds simple and it is to an extent but there is a way to work this so you are successful which we will get into in the coming chapters. We just want you to absorb the gist of what the "Law of Attraction" is.

The only thing you have to know before we go further:

"The Law of Attraction states that what you put out into the Universe as an emotion which to the Universe is the same as intention—it will deliver to you what you want."

Referring to this while you are reading the finer details of this book is imperative to understanding this process. It is just the fundamentals but there is more to it than the statement above and will not work without a full understanding. We will continue explaining this in a way that the lay person who is not fully acquainted with physics or quantum theory. You don't have to be—it is the way each human being experiences life in general except now—you are one of the very fortunate to know the real mechanics and by the end of this book will be able to practice it in your own life.

CHAPTER 2

The Law of Attraction and Religion

"Because you have so little faith. I tell you the truth, if you have faith as small as a mustard seed, you can say to this mountain, 'Move from here to there' and it will move. Nothing will be impossible for you."
- Matthew 17:20

"All things whatsoever ye pray and ask for, believe that ye have received them and ye shall receive them."

There are so many people out there that have attracted valuable information about the "Law of Attraction" and have felt a guilt that has outweighed the drive to actually learn about it. This happens because many are taught that God and if you are Catholic or Christian their Savior Jesus Christ is the one in charge of all the blessings they have and anything outside of that belief is deemed blasphemy.

But alas there are many references in the Bible and other religious books that state that this is something inherent in us that God created and is meant for us to use.

One of those versus is Proverbs 23:7 out of the Christian Bible **"As a man thinketh in his heart so he is"** which says that there is nothing about the Law of Attraction that takes away from any religion. If you carry the belief that there is a God which created us in his own image then it is only respectful to that God to believe that he gave us the inherent ability to live the life we were meant to. When we keep a positive loving emotion, we certainly are emulating the creator so that what we think of as blessing or reward, is just a natural result of our emotions. We are created to create as the creator has. Only, we can't take nothing and make it something—we can take what is already in our lives and attract greatness.

What to remember from this chapter throughout the book:

For those who subscribe to a God or creator of the Universe. We can do this creator no greater service and pay it no greater homage than to reflect a wonderful life. After all—living a life of suffering and resistance to fulfilling our personal purpose would in fact be saying to that creator—"God, you made creations that are unworthy"

Wow, that is a powerful statement. And one that should resonate within the depths of your very soul. So, the best way to serve and love your God is to use the blessing of

Quantum Physics—the movement and formation of matter into your wishes that your created made FOR YOU...

The next chapter will show you how the "Law of Attraction" works and how you can start using it. It will astound you and draw you into a world that you only thought you knew.

CHAPTER 3

How the Law of Attraction Works

"Follow your bliss...
And the universe will open doors where there were only walls."
- Joseph Campbell

As we stated previously, the Law of Attraction is a Law and it is the entitlement of everyone on the planet. We are all made equally in the eyes of the Universe and we are all here to enjoy our lives. This is something that is hard for most people in this society to deal with.

How we are born into the world versus what we are taught once we are here:

When we are born, we are more connected to the Universe, the source of creation than we will most likely ever be in our lives. We are curious, adventurous and bold. Yet, as soon as our protective and well-meaning parents get ahold of us, we are slowly but surely changed into cautious and critical thinking beings. This is because there is an instinct for our parents to protect and mold us into people that can be "ready for the dangers of the world". This in and of itself is not a bad thing—at least not the intention. But, it throws us out of the vibration that we both prior to birth and during life were in. This is the negative thing.

An explanation of vibration:

In order to understand what happens to our ability to create our own reality—we have to explain what a vibration is and what that shift in vibration that we discussed is and how it affects you.

Your vibration is mostly ruled by your emotional state. In simple terms, when you are in a bad or negative mood, then you have a low vibration. When you are in a good mood and thinking positive thoughts, you have a high vibration. Needless to say—it is best to stay in a high vibration. How to do this we will go into in-depth shortly. But first you must understand the basics.

When we are born—we are mostly in a high vibration, pure positive energy state and looking for fun. We don't know any other reality until someone shows us differently and that happens naturally. If you are with positive people, you will maintain that high vibration longer. If you are with negative minded or fearful people you will start to fall into a lower vibration and unless someone shows you how to return to the higher vibration—there you will stay.

How you create your own reality via your vibration:

Thought is actually matter. Though you can't see it until it manifests itself—it is hard to grasp because after all, you are made of matter and so is your dining room table and it is solid. But the wind is also matter and we can't see it. Matter is many things outside your 5 physical senses and they are just as real. You just can't perceive it. Your thoughts and the emotion that you put into those thoughts are actually what create your reality.

So thoughts manifest into physical reality?

Yes they do. Everything your senses pick up around you is in-part a vibrational manifestation of what is active in your mind and emotions somewhere. The one most important yet the most difficult point for people to grasp is this…

You and only you are responsible for everything that happens to you… good or bad—no exceptions.

Because this is such a touchy subject especially since there are a lot of people that have fallen victim to crime and tragedy—we will cover this in-depth first.

First, may we say that we in no way want to make light of anything anyone reading this book has been through. We have all been there. But, we look at this as a gift to you so you can learn what this all means and live the rest of your life the way YOU want it in every way and never be a victim again.

Are you saying that murderers and rapists are not bad people and I "asked" to be victimized? And what about children? How can they be responsible for what happens to them?

First let us say that—no—murderers and rapists should not be excused for victimizing people. After all we did just say that everyone is fully responsible for their actions and reality and this includes them too. But, we will explain how the victim became the victim and how you can avoid such a fate again or at all. Just remember that you may find yourself wanting to teach this to others to "save" them. The best way you can do this is not by words but by your own life or explaining how you do this when you finally get the hang of it—because believe us—you won't want to stop.

How does a victim become a victim and how are they responsible for that?

As you learned earlier—your emotions and thoughts in tandem with one another create your reality. Now, here is the quantum physics of it all which is important. If your thoughts and emotions shape your reality—then whatever manifests is due to what "signal" you put out to the Universe. And yes, it is like a radio signal. You have heard the term "Like attracts like". This is the same, so we will give some examples here.

First let us say that you need to understand in any way you can bring yourself to understand one important and immovable fact:

"The Universe does not run on justice—karma—or any other like philosophy. It only reads your emotions. It doesn't understand good or bad—it is not your friend as some metaphysical movements would like you to believe and it is not your enemy. It is not seeking to reward or punish—it just simply "is".

If you remember this throughout this book you will absorb some very powerful information. You will actually come to embrace it—without too much of a choice as this is not just another metaphysical or religious belief—it is physics—quantum physics—and after reading this book you will become more "awake" to the truths in how the Universe actually works.

Examples of how the Universe works in regard to positive or negative manifestation:

It is not enough to merely say that if you feel in some way like a victim—even subconsciously then the Universe will hear "I am fearful and feel vulnerable and I WANT to be mugged."

But, that IS what it HEARS. It doesn't hear WORDS it FEELS your FEAR even if you are not consciously thinking it. So, the Universe actually reads your fear as what you are actually seeking. Sounds rough but it is the truth.

How it creates your ambush and all the characters that play in it—scenario one:

Picture this—you are going about your business one day and just a few days prior you were discussing with a friend how you are concerned because you moved to the city from the country and you are a female. You don't need to drive in the city, so you are happy that there is public transportation that will save a ton of money—however, you are still nervous about the subway.

Later that week in your new city you get a "sudden inspiration" to get out and about in town to see what the nightlife is about. At the same time there is a maniac that will get the same inspiration to rendezvous with you on the "A" train downtown. You get on and he follows you most of the way home. You walk faster—he walks faster—you turn down a street and so does he. The rest—we will leave to the imagination.

Later, after the mugging—or worse—her friends and family will say things like—wow what a "tragic" or "unlucky" encounter she had. Yes it was tragic and can be seen as unlucky but this is what really happened.

In this girls vibration she put out to the Universe a fear and concern vibration—through this—she told the Universe that she "expected" danger. The Universe said "your wish is my command" and delivered her what she wanted.

What was the mugger's part in it? This is where we teach you what alignment and a vibrational match is.

What is alignment and vibrational match:

In the above example—we said that her fear and concern sent a signal to the Universe that she "expected" danger. The Universe gave her what she "asked" for promptly. And it was done in the form of a vibrational match.

The mugger matched the vibrational signal she gave out so the Universe used synchronicity to provide her with the perfect player in the ambush.

Now, are we defending the mugger? No. But, she was a co-creator of that event, needs to change her vibration now and make sure that now that she has become a victim—she does not perpetuate it even more.

Perpetuating a low vibration through therapy:

In this society we are forced into therapy or at least seeking the help of family and friends to help us through what just happened. This, in and of itself is not a bad thing initially. But, the longer you stay on a subject the more "fuel" you give the victim vibration and before you know it—it has happened again.

Ever hear the cliché why do bad things happen to good people? This is why. Because it has nothing to do with how "good" of a person you are. It has to do with what signal you are putting out—plain and simple. So, regarding therapy—go if you must—talk to people but be mindful to be positive and focus upon what you want and not what you don't want which we will cover shortly.

Example of achieving manifestation of good things through high vibration—scenario two:

Again a man—Mr Jones we'll call him walks around with gratitude on his heart for everything he does have. He is an outgoing gentleman that sees himself as safe and successful. People love him but they envy him as well. Everyone knows someone like this—the "lucky" ones.

Example of achieving positive manifestation through high vibration even if you are a criminal—scenario three:

In this instance—Mr Jones can also be a con artist—a swindler of other people's money and yet be the "luckiest" person on earth. So you say? How can that be that Mr Jones the criminal gets away with what he does—is there no justice?

Not in the Universe there isn't

There is only vibrational signals and matches. If Mr. Jones has no fear, only confidence, no guilt, only self-serving justification, and no remorse then the Universe will continue to put the best people—including the victims that we discussed earlier as the best vibrational match for Mr. Jones to take full advantage of.

Yes, we agree as humans writing this book that this seems really rough. But this is the answer to those that ask the creator they believed created them "why when I am a good person that does the right thing do I get crapped on from great height?"

"Why do you not protect me?"

The answer is, "Because I created you with free will and I already said a thousand times if I said it once—as a man thinketh in his heart so he is"

So let's move forward after the recap shall we and try to change what we thinketh in our hearts to a greater life.

RECAP CHAPTERS 1, 2, 3

*H*ere we will briefly recap what we have learned so far. It is our suggestion that you take the time to digest these points and even go back and look at the points prior to moving forward. If you have anyone that wants to learn this—you may want to have them read the book to or give it to them as a gift so that you may partner with them in the knowledge and strengthen each other's weak points in the knowledge.

Points to Remember:

- **Everyone is entitled by this Law to have what they want:** This point taught you that this is simply a Law that everyone has the right to benefit from. It has nothing to do with punishment or blessing and has nothing to do with how good of a person you are or not. It is a law of physics like gravity.

- **You are responsible for everything that manifests its way into your life:** You should understand by this point that you are the sole person who is responsible for what comes to you good or bad—positive or negative. You understand that the Universe is not a friend or foe. It is just a means of moving and manifesting matter through your emotions that are crafted by your thoughts.

- **The Universe does not read thoughts or words:** Your emotions are the only thing that the Universe reads. You may facilitate your emotions with your thoughts but your thoughts are only a guide used by you to bring up emotions. Like looking at a butterfly brings emotions of being happy.

- **Alignment and Vibrational Match:** You understand by this post that you are a vibrational match to whatever you are attracting into your life or it wouldn't be there in the first place.

CHAPTER 4

Resistance

"Whether you think you can or whether you think you can't, you're right."
- **Henry Ford**

$\mathcal{N}$ow that you have those crucial points down—you will learn one of the most important things. The part that resistance plays in our manifestation process. It is nothing to be frustrated or to feel "wrong" about because we create resistance by default without even knowing it. Ah, but when you practice it, long enough you will start to catch yourself doing it.

Creating Resistance and How to Spot it:

So, what is resistance? Resistance is just a part of the way we think. In order to manifest something we want we need to think of ONLY what we WANT and NOT what we DONT WANT. But, very often when thinking of what we want we're actually focusing on the "opposite side of the stick" – the lack of what we want.

When we do that—we send an equal signal to the Universe to send more of the lack, more of the "not having-ness" to us and in fact—cause a block to what we want at the same time we are sending a signal out to send us what we want. Confusing huh? Yup, it is, but you will see it much more clearly very shortly.

Black Horse White Horse

The example we use to describe resistance is a picture of a race track with only two horses racing. The white horse which represents positive emotion reaching out for what you really want in a positive way. The other black horse represents the negative or resistant emotion.

Now, how the race goes is up to you. You can move the horses any way you want to with whatever emotion you put into it. So, what does that look like?

When you put what you want in a positive way for example—"I want more money" and you are then allowing your white horse to gain momentum to the finish line. But, when you state "I want more money BECAUSE I am really sick of not having it" and you put your focus on the lack of money in your life. This is when your black horse gains just as much momentum to the finish line.

The finish line represents your manifestation and what you get back is a GRAY horse. Meaning a mixed bag of manifestation. You have successfully manifested both having it and not having it.

What this process actually does is slow down the manifestation of what you really want. This causes immense frustration and depression which only keeps you on the wrong level of vibration.

So what does the gray horse look like?

This is an example of what the gray horse looks like. You manifest five dollars that you find in a coat pocket and then get upset because you asked for 500. The reason you only got five dollars is because you put it out that you wanted money but also gave the emotion of lacking money so...you got the money on a small scale.

Why People Slip Into the Bad Vibe:

We are human. That would be the short answer. But, there are deliberate reasons why we slip into the negative. Basically it is our conditioning that we have had since birth. We are taught things like, we have to work hard for money and if we don't we're lazy. Many adopt the belief that "success is difficult". We are taught if you ask God to help you, you have to proclaim it as if it is the will of God that you are healthy or prosperous in any way. This means that we give our power away. You are already equipped with the ability to manifest things you want and need from the divine because you are part of the divine. Our attitude and belief systems about this are what mess us up. We are taught to think we are somehow below the creator and less deserving unless the divine power we worship gives us some kind of permission to accept "gifts". These "gifts" are already an entitlement for us when we come here and manifest bodies.

Why "contrast" is necessary in your life experience:

A certain amount of resistance and unwanted experiences (also known as "contrast") is necessary in your life. Contrast clarifies what you do want and what you don't want. Contrast then makes you create new desires within in you. This is the way the world is constructed – for you to constantly create new desires and move toward them.

Why we are Actually Here:

Most people have an issue with the reason why we are here. We feel we are beholden to others and we have to always help others and take less for ourselves. This is why our bodies are in a state of disease or **DIS**-EASE. Cancer and fibromyalgia and a lot of other stress-related illnesses come from the fact that we believe we must give 24 hours a day and 7 days a week or we are not a good person, or not a good mother or not a good friend or teacher etc...

There are a lot of beliefs that we have around why we are here. We believe that we are here for others and for the planet and for the job we have and to sacrifice like a saint or martyr. Look at the basis for some religions of the world. They are based on overall good things like charity, service and good will.

This is not a bad thing overall but when we place our whole identity in these things and then feel that we have failed—guess what? We are at a low vibe and what's worse is it means that other people are ruling our emotions and what do our emotions represent? Our vibration. And what does our vibration represent? It represents what we manifest.

So, why are we Really Here?

For the experience of physical reality and expansion as well as pleasurable feelings such as joy, excitement and exhilaration. That would be the short answer. It is also an intrinsically selfish answer. This would be taken as negative by most of society but it shouldn't be. Here we will go through how to view yourself as who you really are and then give you a better understanding as to why we tell you that you are here to please yourself.

The Soul's Journey through the Earth Plane:

Most people apart from maybe an atheist will understand the concept that we have a soul or spirit and we have a body to encase it for the earth plane. The soul is not made as a service vessel for society. It is here to "experience". The experience is needed to "enjoy" life. Yes this means to do whatever you want to do to make yourself happy first. Now, if that means serving others makes you happy then that is what you do but if it doesn't make you happy—then think of what does, and do it. This is more easily said than done. This is because everything we do as a human being to support those body's like work and school and parenthood and such—will be bombarding you with the opposite. But once you have made the commitment to really live for you first—the manifestations will take care of everything.

The Job of the Soul:

The job of the soul is to experience everything it chose to experience on the Earth plane. It can choose parents and all kinds of circumstances but not a choice as we think of it between this and that. It is still vibrational attraction. Whatever vibration your soul is in when you are ready to be born—then that is what you attract to you as far as parents and circumstances but you don't choose the entire specifics of your lifetime because you will attract your experiences vibrationally as you go. Just as you attracted this book—you will attract all your experiences and all the people around you good or bad until you die. After death the same thing happens you may or may not come back—you will attract other souls and circumstances just as you always have. This takes us to the lesson in being in the now and that there is only now. We will explain that in more detail next as well as the concept that you are never really finished.

Being in the Now in Relation to Manifestation:

When you are living in the now, it means you are not obsessing over the past or the future. It means you are in the best space to manifest anything you want with a clean stream of energy. If you are in the past, you are forever ruminating over something that has been done and you are creating more momentum toward that. If you recall what we said about momentum in an earlier chapter—you will see that the more energy you place toward something, the stronger it gets. That means that you cannot deactivate what you started and it just keeps drawing you backward. This makes it not impossible but not easy by any stretch of the imagination to create a future without dragging that past momentum with you. Here is an example.

Letting go of the "How" Concept:

This is one of the most important concepts for LOA. This is what causes most of the resistance—even more than fear or doubt and that is "how". We are so used to being the thinking, doing, conquering control freaks. When we want something, we normally start the mapping of how we will do the manifesting of what we want.

Example of Letting go of the "How":

You want money. You want several streams of income. So, you decide to sit down and plan how you will conquer it, nail it down and work toward it. Then, confusion and frustration sets in because some of your plans go awry. This is now creating resistance that will eventually pull in the "White Horse- Gray Horse" effect we are talking about.

The primary reason to let go of how to obtain or acquire a thing or circumstance is that you will be taking the trust away from the Universe and rendering it useless to you.

Example:

When you take a bit too much action to obtain something you are in effect not waiting for your best options to be presented to you. You are in effect carving out a path that you "think" is correct. When you are being guided by the Universe and quantum physics, you are "feeling" it is the right path to take to achieve your goal.

Path of Least Resistance:

When you are already confused and frustrated—you are essentially closing off doors to pathways that are the "Paths of Least Resistance". The Universe is already well-versed in the way of the path that will bring you to where you need to be to get what you want. It is a simple concept that is so simple—we doubt it. This is a major blockage to manifestation.

When you start putting out the vibration of how you will obtain something you also subtly do something else as well. As you are visualizing the plan of action to take to achieve what you want—you are in effect—offering a vibration for each of the steps you "think" you need to take. When this happens—the Universe has to—by law—rearrange molecules in your reality to make the steps you thought of possible.

Whereas—if you would have dwelt on the end result only—the Universe would have been set free to rearrange molecules to the path of least resistance—but noooooo we all have to stand in our own way—don't we?

A little humor there but it hits home. We are so afraid to let go that we stand literally in our own way so, let's learn to stop doing that with a little practice shall we?

Example of Momentum:

You were fired from a job under bad circumstances. You feel like you were treated unfairly and it did a number on your confidence. You really want a new job but, you can't seem to stop thinking of what happened in the last job. This is an example of creating momentum. According to quantum physics—if you spend just under a minute thinking of something—then it has enough momentum to reach out and attract matching thoughts and circumstances. So, this makes it very hard to reach out and create something different. Again, it isn't impossible and we will teach you this in the work book as well.

The good news is that good momentum acts the same way and that means better manifestation for what you want. For now we will exit this concept and go into a little about the fact that you never really get it all done.

We Never Get It Done? Please Do Explain.

The best example that can be given is when we set goals especially goals that are for a certain time period to be fulfilled. It is a hard thing for people to wrap their heads around, accept it and relax in that knowingness. People can understand the concept when they have it explained as we will do here but the issue is rarely understanding but accepting. This is again due to the way we are brought up.

We went into this a bit in other chapters but it is necessary to cover it more than once because this is a concept that is quite vast and our upbringing will affect it on every count.

Where we are when we are Born:

When we are born we are far more who we are supposed to be. We are much closer to our true selves. This means we explore without fear and with much curiosity. But, through our parents and our surroundings we are marred and brought into a fearful space. We become more aware of the dangers of our surroundings and we are—in this society—watched with our children more than at any other time. We are told that if we aren't perfect with them and they are not encased in plastic—that we are bad parents and can even be sent to jail or have our children taken away.

So, what does that do to a child's vibration? It makes it so much lower and begins attracting things out of fear. Unfortunately, it is one of those things that is the more sensitive areas to discuss. This is explained in the section that covered why bad things happen to good people and why bad people have great things happen to them.

Remember that the Universe has no sense of justice—only creation from your vibration and though you can't create in that child's reality, you can in fact influence the way they think and feel—hence—they will act think and feel accordingly and this is how their lives are structured.

Back to Never Getting it Done:

We wanted you to understand the concept of what space you are in when you are born so this part would be easier. As we travel along in our life—we allow people and circumstances to influence us greatly. One way that people and circumstances influence us is in what we think we need to do and accomplish in a certain period of time and throughout a lifetime.

Example:

"I have to have a certain career and earn a certain amount of money in order to be a worthy person"

Wow, that is a LOT of pressure. But, this is learned beliefs. When we believe this way, we are bucking our own current. We are creating resistance to what we want out of life—even the very thing such as this "career" that we think we need.

The truth is we never stop wanting and we never stop planning and doing. We never stop attempting to get what we want and what we want changes. This is a natural progression in things and what happens is, we tend to fight our nature. We are afraid that our friends and family will call us lazy and unmotivated or on the flip side-- a workaholic or unstable when we move from thing to thing. But this is what we were meant to do in order to expand the soul.

The soul's primary purpose is to expand, experience and discover so there is really no such thing as you make a goal—achieve it and then that is where it ends. But here is where it gets even more complicated.

We think in terms of doing the "right thing" a lot so after reading this section—you may think well what am

I SUPPOSED to do? Am I supposed to have a career? Am I supposed to have kids? Get married? Stay single? And the list goes on and on and on.

But the truth is—you are to do what makes you happy at the time. And here is the next clincher—if it hurts someone—so be it!

We aren't suggesting that you go off and just tear people up. We suggest you love everyone—just don't live to please everyone—including your society that makes everything just so complicated!

Aren't we Supposed to be there for Each Other?

The answer to that is this...Yes and No. A good analogy is as follows – in an airplane the flight attendant tells you to **put on your breathing mask before helping anyone else.** You have to take care of yourself first (from a "thinking/energetic" point of view) because you have nothing to give to others if you don't.

But this is a deep one and there's much more to it so take a quick break and come back when you are refreshed!

OK, welcome back and we hope you are refreshed!

In effect, we are made to—as we said—expand ourselves. If being there for others is part and parcel of that expansion then so be it. But in saying that—if being there for others means that it affects our way of thinking which in-turn taints our emotions—which in turn taints our manifestation process—then no should not be there for that person.

When cutting ties gets hard:

So, with so many millions of people with codependency issues—how do we make them superior manifesters without them cracking up? The good news is—the way other people act around us is also part and parcel of what vibrational frequency we are on.

We stated earlier when we spoke about children and the influence our parents have on our vibration when we are little, that we cannot create in another person's reality. But, we also said that our influence is great on their vibration. So, sure, you can be there for someone and help them out without dragging yourself down. It is a win-win situation if you do it right and here we will teach you how to train your vibration to stay where it is regardless of what anyone else is doing or what the circumstances are. And we will also teach you how to only meet up with a person when they are on a higher vibration and meet the best part of that person and not the worst part.

CHAPTER 5

Training Your Vibration and Attraction

"Change the way you look at things and the things you look at change."
- **Wayne Dyer**

OK, we are at the point now where we just discussed and digested a bit about being selfish and being there for people. You are probably just at the point of thinking that you are such a giving person, you could never just turn away from anyone ever. When it comes to family—you are the one that's there—when it comes to friends—you are the one that's there. But as we promised—we are going to be able to tell you here how to handle it all in two ways. Let's recap for a moment the Law of Attraction so that it is fresh in your head.

The Law of Attraction means that like attracts like. The Universe only reads emotions and that is the way you tell it what you want. The Universe always delivers. If you are in a negative mood and worried then you will attract those people who are in the same energetic state.

There is more to it but this is the part regarding being there for people so let's just focus on that for this chapter. OK, so let's say for example you have a person in the family that you can't make happy no matter what you do. They are simply addicted to drama and despite your greatest efforts—you can't change it because they don't want to change it.

The First Tough Part:

Now, knowing that you only attract what you have in your own vibration—this means—that this person is a mirror to you and you to them. This means that the only person you need to look at is yourself first. You may want to complain that this person is always around you this way bringing you down—but—this person could not physically be around you if there wasn't either one of two things alive in your vibration.

1.) Either you are the same exact type of person in some way..or..

2.) You have a victim or complaining mentality.

It doesn't even have to be conscious or exaggerated. It just has to be there somewhere. So, this makes us fully responsible for what and who we attract to us. So, what's the remedy? The two things we will discuss next is how to do it and in the workbook section is where we will get to teach you some exercises to enable you to make it all a habit.

First Solution to the Problem:

The first solution to the problem is to train your vibration to stay in the same, high range. From the moment you wake up in the morning—you are setting your vibrational tone for the entire day. If you went to bed in a good mood or a bad mood you usually wake up the same way. So, it is best you start meditating in the morning and practice setting the tone to the best possible vibration.

Step two is, practice keeping yourself in the same vibration all day long regardless of what is going on. Now, we don't expect miracles so this is what you do: at the beginning of the day you set the tone and then when you come across someone or something that is in the opposite vibration, you will catch yourself and keep your vibration stable by thinking of something pleasant.

We will go through this in the workbook a bit deeper and really show you how to do it. But, it is essential that you know now that you never think to yourself any thought of RESISTING your friend who Is in a negative state or a circumstance that is not your best. This just makes things worse and will strengthen the negative vibe. When this happens you will snowball your day full of the same occurrences and people until you are pulling your hair out.

So, this is also a good example of momentum as well. By catching your thoughts under a minute, you can avoid momentum and all it brings with it when it is a bad thought. Same goes for a good thought in which case you want to really dwell on the person or the occurrence because it is a good momentum.

The Second Solution to the Problem:

The second solution to the problem is to raise your own vibration and visualize with emotion the person so you will attract the best parts of that person. This we will explain. When you meet up with someone on the street, you will already be a vibrational match to them in some way. When you decide that you are happy and upbeat and all is right in the world and maintain that for long enough a time and keep building on that—you will match up with the person that has been driving you nuts—but—ONLY when they are matched to YOU. SO you only get them on their good days. And eventually you may just rub off on them.

Both steps take time to practice but after a while you will understand that it is a simple concept of like attracts like. In fact—this entire book—is about that one line—those three words. You see how just our belief system keeps us from doing such a simple thing. We hope that just knowing that will bolster your determination to learn this and become able to control your vibration so you can create a spectacular life.

CONCLUSION

At this point, we will again recap all five chapters so you can do several things. One, is so that you have some understanding of how the Law of Attraction works. From here on, we will refer to it as LOA in the workbook. The second thing the recap is for is so you can review anything you don't understand and continue to review it until you do. Please feel free to comment on the website and ask questions. The more feedback we get, the better your LOA learning experience will be.

RECAP OF CHAPTERS 1-5

$\mathcal{T}$he first five chapters we went through took us through what the LOA is. How it works and how to make sure you are not creating resistance or holding on to the "How" concept.

- **Like Attracts Like:** It was described as a law that is as natural as the law of gravity. It is simply put- like attracts like. You also learned that the Universe does not read thoughts but emotions. You use visualization to enhance the

- **Not Creating Resistance:** This was explained in examples of thinking and feeling what you want without including resistance. This meant only sending a clean stream of what you want—not what you don't want.

- **Letting Go of "How":** You learned how to be rid of the limiting beliefs that create resistance and hold back manifestation. You also learned how to uncomplicate the manifestation process.

If there are any of these sections that you do not feel comfortable with—we suggest that you go back to them and recap them yourself. In the space below, write down any and all questions and thoughts so you can also refer to the website for some further answers and guidance. This book is pretty comprehensive and we are going to make sure that you have the tools to practice LOA and see the manifestations in your own life as soon as possible when it is executed correctly and approached honestly.

YOUR FREE WORKBOOK

"Everything you want is out there waiting for you to ask. Everything you want also wants you. But you have to take action to get it."
- Jack Canfield

In this section, you will learn how to actually put the concepts in the material into practice. Now that you have taken a much-needed break from the recap we can move forward and allow you to experience what an awesome life you can have when you learn the habit of the LOA! This will be a simple and easy section that won't be miles long with way too much impractical exercise to actually do.

What we have to Actually Practice

This is where—with a great attitude—you may take a breath and rest a bit. This is because what you have to actually "practice" is not much at all—it can just be done in different ways. Here we will concentrate on several small steps and also several traits we must develop in ourselves.

EXERCISE ONE: LIVING IN THE NOW

$\mathcal{T}$his is a logical first exercise because if we are focused on the past or the future we will create resistance.

Things you can do to live in the now:

1. **Take a walk and concentrate on objects in nature:** Start here first because it is a more relaxing canvass to work on. You can practice simple meditation while there are no great distractions.

2. **Talk to yourself:** This may seem a bit hokey and make you feel kinda crazy but it works. Wherever you are and whatever you are doing—make positive statements about what you are doing. This does two things. First, it will program your mind for the positive and teach it to reach out and attract more positive thoughts. The second

thing it will do is distract us from the past, future or any planning or obsessing over what we want. This will get you out of your own way and pave the way to getting your desire fulfilled.

Example:

While you are washing dishes say "I am really enjoying washing the dishes and feeling the warm water on my hands". If you are alone and it is quiet which is the most dangerous time for most people to start thinking and creating resistance—we should say something like…" wow I am so grateful that I get this quiet time" "I am so grateful to live where I live and get a great day off like this"

You get the idea now? It is simply practicing focus to distract yourself from what you don't want to think of. It takes at least 3 weeks to learn a new habit and to reprogram the actual cells in your body to start thinking a different way.

EXERCISE 2:
STAYING IN A NEUTRAL STATE

*T*he next logical thing to learn is to stay in a neutral state of thought about your desire. This is another way to get out of your way and not restrict the Universe while it does its work.

How to stay in a neutral state:

1. **Quick Switch of Thoughts:** Whenever you feel you can't have a positive emotion about your desire or you doubt the fact that you can get it then do a quick switch of thoughts. This means totally and completely neutral thoughts.

Example:

You get up one morning in a deep blue funk about your situation. You started momentum on it the night before and though you stopped the general momentum while asleep—you have begun it again. To stop this takes a simple action that is a lot of the time more easily said than done.

Turn your thoughts to something very neutral and benevolent. Go back to the same thought style and similar subjects that we gave you in the "Living in the Now" section. Again—three weeks and you'll be doing this on autopilot.

EXERCISE 3:
STAYING IN YOUR VIBRATION

This is probably the most difficult one to learn because we are very defensive and easily taken in by other people's moods and vibrations. The key to staying in your own vibration is practice of the first two steps. Yes, you may have to know how to either politely change the subject that someone is on or you may have to have a conversation and tell the person you will listed but will not allow them to rile you up in any way. It is not that you don't care—but the misery loves company rout is not for you.

Once you have practiced the first two exercises enough—you will not have this third issue anymore or at least far less. And when you do spot it—you'll be able to stop it. This is because, as we explained—your vibration will not match those people so you should not meet up with them.

Example:

Try to think of the person or situation that you want your vibe to match and start acting the part. Like an actor on the screen, you have a character to build and the more emotion and belief you have going towards that character—the more the Universe will move those molecules around for you again and you will not run into the people that do not match your vibration.

EXERCISE 4:
EFFORTLESS MANIFESTATION

Once you are practicing all the three steps we have just listed, you will be able to start practicing the easiest exercise to effortless manifestation. This does not even need an example. It is simply to dwell only on the end result and feel the victory and what it feels like to have it.

It seems almost ludicrous to have an instruction manual for something that only needs one step. But it is necessary because for human beings at their very core—it is near impossible for us to dwell on an end result we think—or better yet—we feel will never happen. This manual is all about getting the self-esteem, confidence and positive attitude to succeed at this. It is our own sabotaging attitudes that make our vibration take a nose dive.

Example:

Wanna get married? Then you should feel the way you would feel being married. If you want a car—then feel the way you would feel driving it. If you need to, buy some of that new car smell spray and spray it in your room or better yet—your old car. This is because you need to really feel it. When you are driving your car—feel how you would feel if you were in it already.

Buy something that represents what you want and wear it or use it or have it around you. When you want to travel—get the luggage and keep it out and look at it. Wanna go to France? Play french music and eat french food and maybe start studying the language. Go into it as much as you can to make it all real to you. Once you start getting excited about it all—you are giving the Universe permission to move those molecules to bring the form that you want.

Hopefully it won't be full of resistance and you won't be letting the white horse and black horse out of the gate again together. Or, if you do, you may want to make sure the white horse is more than a length ahead.

EXERCISE 6: TIMING

Timing is everything. According to quantum physics and its authorities on the subject—if you spend less than 20 seconds on a thought it will gain momentum. If you spend more than that—it will start moving into manifestation fast. Let's face it—when we want something and we are fearful—we will spend days on a thought—much less 20 seconds or less. So, we need to be cognizant of the timing that we spend on a good or bad thought. We certainly want to spend as much time as possible on a good thought because we want that momentum but the bad thoughts.. no. They need to be stopped as soon as we start thinking of it.

CONCLUSION

Technically, all you need is number 6 to accomplish effortless manifestation. But because we are human we need them all. In the next section—we will address some of the questions that may be going through your head and see if we can answer some of those questions that we can anticipate.

FAQS PAGE

Do I have to now monitor all my thoughts? Sounds like too much work. :

This is probably the most frequently asked questions. When we begin to explain resistance—people are scared that they will have to watch every thought they have. And while that is true to an extent – I would call it more of a "guiding" process. What you really have to monitor is your feelings – you should be reaching for a better feeling all the time. What you also have to keep in mind is that law of attraction doesn't allow leaps in vibration, meaning that you cannot instantly go from a negative feeling to a positive one. You can only gradually "climb up the feeling ladder." For example: going from bad feelings like sadness to more neutral ones like contentment to positive ones like happiness and joy.

How do I deactivate the bad momentum?:

You can never destroy a thought because you can't destroy matter which is what a thought is. But you can activate new momentum so that the old momentum loses steam.

Do I have to renounce my religion to practice this? Is it a sin?:

Not on both counts. First, this is complimentary to your religion. You are not worshiping anything. You are simply managing your thoughts to achieve a better life and result in that life. Most religion teaches how to do this anyway through prayer and other methods. It is not a sin because we are not dealing with gods—we are practicing this everyday like it or not actually. This is a law just like the law of gravity. Remember that in the dark ages and prior to that—people thought many scientific beliefs were of the devil. You were a heretic if you believed what the church and other religions now readily accept. In fact, if you listen to most Christian preachers they actually teach a principle called "Prosperity Preaching" They repeat over and over again to "name it and claim it" it doesn't matter that it is in the name of God or not. If you are an avid prayer, and you feel you deserve what you are getting then you will have it simply because your emotions are being read and if you believe it—your god is answering you. Ever notice that sometimes when people prayed for good health or a healing for a loved one—that some are saved and some are not? This is not because there is a god that only favors some. It is directly related to the vibration and the feelings that the dying person and the family is offering. Remember, every religion tells us we were made with free will when we live or die can be our choice as well.

How do I stop sabotaging my manifestations?:

You simply need to practice the exercises in this book and make sure you are not frustrated while doing it. It takes time but eventually you will master it.

What do I do about non-believers?:

As you get more and more involved in understanding these principles—will start becoming more sensitive to the energy of the people around us. This can be scary because if the people around us notice a change as big as this one—you may have some relationship and social issues to deal with. We won't lie and tell you that you may not lose some friendships or at least they will change. However, you can choose to manifest those that are of like mind or stay around those who will continue to drag misfortune to them. Now, if you have fairly positive friends to begin with—they should actually accept your beliefs. If they are concerned about your religion—then explain number 3 in this section to them. If they still don't let up then you may choose to handle it the way we will explain next. But remember, if they leave on their own accord it just means that for now, you are not a vibrational match for them and that is OK.

How to share this with those closest to you:

Honestly this does not have to be that hard. In order to share this with those closest to you—you don't have to explain the whole quantum physics science with them. They will probably only look at you like you have two heads and may even suggest mental help. So, instead of subjecting yourself to this sort of thing—you have to teach by example and let them come to you. You will find just naturally that people will ask you how you seem to have an easy life and they may even be jealous of you. They will be looking at very one dimensional, practical reasons for your success. They may accuse you or suspect you of things as well. After all, if you are all of a sudden manifesting money left and right—you may get a few raised eyebrows. But we hope that you are manifesting the heck out of life and if you do so without fear, you will be protected against any onslaughts. But if you manifest with guilt or fear you will be subject to even more of it. Remember the principles!

So, in order to safely teach people why you are as "lucky" as you are—you will have to respond with what you do and what attitude you have. For example—your friend says wow you seem to get job offers galore! What are you doing? You have hardly left the house and I know you haven't applied on line much you would have told me! So, what gives?

What your response should be is that you are a people person and your contacts have come to you. Tell them you also notice that "somehow" when you get more attention regarding what you want when you meditate first or when you are less stressed. Eventually they will become a vibrational match to you and succeed themselves or they will make their way out of your life. Whether that is a permanent situation or not only time will tell.

FINAL WORDS

*"What you are is what you have been.
Who you will be is what you do now."*
- Buddha

This book was put together to help elevate the human race and assist in its evolution at a time that we feel people are ready. It seems we are in the right time because even those that are conservative in their beliefs are open minded enough to at least let it in a little.

Our governments and scientists can no longer deny that there are laws in this Universe that give the human being much more control over their own destiny. It has been kept to the 1% which rules the world and kept from us for far too long. Go forward is knowledge and peace my friends.

www.ingramcontent.com/pod-product-compliance
Lightning Source LLC
Chambersburg PA
CBHW052205110526
44591CB00012B/2092